Pages From

Her Life

Pages From Her Life
by Anindita Rath
Paperback Edition

First Published in 2023 by

Inkfeathers Publishing
Vivek Vihar, New Delhi 110095
www.inkfeathers.com

ISBN 9788119483280

Pages From
Her Life

Anindita Rath

Inkfeathers Publishing
www.inkfeathers.com

dedicated to

I am deeply grateful to the amazing people who stood by me throughout my writing journey. Your support and encouragement have been my driving force, filling my heart with warmth every time my words touched someone's soul.

My heartfelt thanks to my parents, Mr. Satyanarayan Rath and Mrs. Laxmiprava Mishra, my unwavering pillars of strength. They transformed my stubbornness into resilience and my moodiness into creativity. Their constant support and love have been my guiding light, shaping me into the person I am today. Their dedication to their passions has been a source of inspiration, teaching me the value of perseverance and dedication. And my brother Abhilas Rath who has always been a support in the times I want to vent out my feelings and adding a fun element to my life.

I am also thankful to the Almighty, whose divine presence has been a ray of light in my life. In moments of confusion and darkness, your guidance has been my solace. Your unwavering support has protected me, guiding me toward the right path and inspiring me to pursue my dreams fearlessly.

To everyone who has played a part in my journey, thank you for being my source of strength and inspiration. This book is as much yours as it is mine, and I dedicate it to each one of you who believed in me and my words.

contents

the verdicts

the heartbreaks

the emptiness

she took it all in, she broke

she stood alone

she made herself a palace

from the broken pieces

her journey became

a work of art

for all those who watched

the family

the starry night

evening sun has set
the ray of light
on the door
is yet to disappear

looked like a sky
full of stars
blinking
one after the other

night came knocking
soon after
fireflics went wild
making the trees glow

the dance of joy
embarked
brightly moon joined in
ready to take a bow

laid the carpet
of cherry blossoms
splendid spring
nature went euphoric

fell on earth
cocooned with love
blinking her little eyes
like a starry night

out of mother's womb

holding her little feet
in her hand that day
a mother's eyes were stuck
on her baby doll,
with tears of emotions, freshly born.

envisioning her future
pondering on the numbers
the moments she might need to mold,
in the life's journey.

kissing her little feet
wondering about the paths ahead,
for the little soul
enduring trials that she had faced
in the life's brawl

mother's soft whispers

the mother had
let her to be
whoever she wants to be

letting her explore
the way through life
teaching her to fight
for the things she deserve
no less than others

"the world is never fair"
told the mother
the young child
could not quite catch the essence
asking millions of questions

the mother knew
its beyond her comprehension
all she wanted to
tell her what all is out there
for her
before it's too late!

- to my fierce mother

journey of little steps

her little steps unstoppable
ambition and intrigue
were her acquaintance
she aspired to write her own life's page.

each day, new dreams she saw,
wishing to go on the paths untraveled,
desiring to journey far,
to achieve,
with tender feet and aspirations untamed.

to be born or not

"a girl's a burden," they said,
before she was even born
her destiny they decided

not wanting her
wishing her
to be a boy they prayed
who can look after them
to care for them as they aged

they have to
get her married
and dowries need to be paid
that's all
their little minds weighed

patriarchy is what
had them in claws
they were absolved
in the sweet poison of money
drowning in the
deep see of greed
their souls were lost

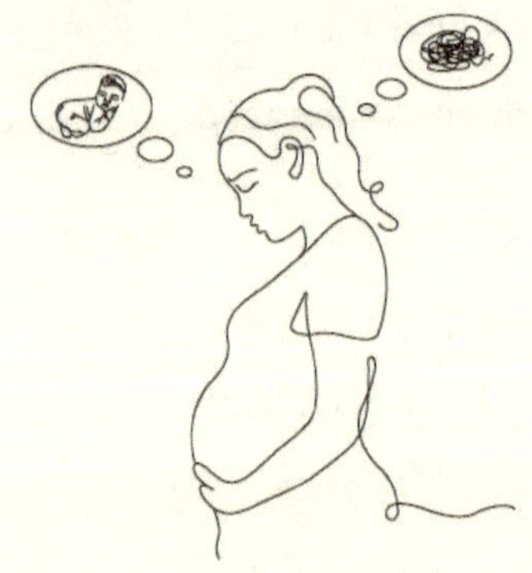

the pink sweater

She was looking at the bright pink sweater that her best friend was wearing. Appreciating the detailed embroidered colourful work on hands. The big white buttons on the front was adding a contrast colour to it.

Looked at her pale clothes broke her heart that day, she hurried home from school to her mother, telling her all about it.

The momentary silence of her mother followed after. Her mother promised she will get it next year for her birthday. Though unspoken, she somehow understood the pain behind her smile of not able to fulfil her wish.

It so happened that the little girl became a lot older that day when she whispered her mother while cuddling her to sleep "Mom, you know, I'm not that fond of pink anyway. Maybe green or yellow. Plus, the one I already have is pretty good, right? It's lasted for two years. Maybe, we can find something for you on your next birthday... Maybe even a pink sweater!""

daddy's precious girl

he works hard
every day,
to give her what
he never had.

he lets her be free
yet keeps her safe
in his own way.

he lets her dream
the mountains unreach
to explore
the endless sky,
that's where you learn
to live your life from
he always say.

he watches her
grow up
to be the woman
he hoped she'd be.
he sees her
facing her own problems
and staying strong
no matter what comes her way.

she's wanted to
be like her dad,
dreaming
one day she could fulfill
all his abandoned dreams,
given up providing her desires.

she sees a little reflection of him
in her as she grows up
not a reflection anymore, everyone said
she is exactly
like her dad

-darling daughter to daring father

love interpretation

she watched her mom
trapped in the kitchen
often
coming out just to eat
when it's time for others to sleep

her mom smiled every time
she asked
for a late-night snack
rushing to the kitchen
to find some food

moms are made of
some unique essence
can sacrifice her life for a child
when circumstance dictate.

but why must she,
be celebrated solely for sacrifice?
isn't she a human too,
entitled to her own rights?

yet, she eats the rest,
with a contented heart,
believing it to be love.
with no complaints
no expectations
to get what she deserve

but is it genuinely love?
or is it simply societal pressure,
to become a hero who relinquishes all,
before being an individual?

the betting game

she grew up
having a little child
in the house
pampered,
soaked with love and care

she had a friend always
to laugh with
or even to fight
loved their little chat
on the way back home,
and him holding her finger
dragging her to places
that makes him wander

the love he got
was not she felt bad about
it's the choices that she had
was the toughest

where the boy has
the realm of choices,
or even the liberty,
to restrain from choosing entirely.

its later when she knew
unaware of the biased love
the freedom of his actions
without thinking the aftermath,
yet he remained unaware
of the prejudice
that he always had the higher bet

-to the patriarchal thoughts

hidden loved toy

the favourite toy
always by her side
a friend in joy
all her secrets
she would confide

on that fateful day
her grasp did falter, and it slip away,
crying for hours
to get it fixed again
her dreadful eyes that day
displayed the loss of a loved one

still she kept it
a souvenir of love's first goodbye
little did she know, as she held each part,
more heartbreaks would find way
to her fragile heart.

it stayed with her for years
witnessing her journey
a token of resilience amidst the tears
that toy, once shattered, now made her strong,
in its broken pieces,
she found where she belonged.

beyond gender's bias

they live together
in the same house,
not so different
somewhat similar

stories they share
for each other
they care,
laugh at silly things
and fight the next moment,
differ in opinions
yet share the one left chocolate

he's like a version of her, you see,
just the way she hoped he'd be.
he's meant to shield her, they say,
from the world, come what may.

but she doesn't need his protection,

neither does he.

side by side, they can stand,

she looks out for him, and he'll do the same,

no matter what.

it isn't about the boy or girl,
it's about the emotions they share

being there for each other

not because

they owe one another

youth's silent vow

her body grew and changed,
from cute frocks,
she moved at last.
advised to hide herself as if a crime,
her innocence lost in this time.

inside, she remained just the same,
those gazes on her played
feeling of being caged,
some stared at her chest, her size,
with their leering eyes.

confused, it must be her fault,
ignored the judgements on her way
why judge her body, she'd often say.

why the shift in how they see?
her body's not a mystery.
innocence lost,
her heart would ache,
let her be herself, let her body be free.

ten thousand questions

Youth came knocking, a mountain of questions invaded her thoughts. Each query, like a fragile thread, remained sealed within her, too delicate to come out. Her new womanhood brought with it a bunch of uncertainties, questions she was too timid to voice or even ponder in the quiet of her solitude.

With the advent of her monthly cycle, her fear reached their peak. The sight of fluid coming out of her body gave her nightmares, a fear that persisted for several months before transforming into acceptance of its normalcy.

Those initial nights were plagued by sleeplessness, consumed by the anxiety of staining her sheets, haunted by the notion of morning embarrassment. The fear of someone noticing the mark on her dress maybe.

In her fragile teenage years, she left the comfort of her mother's presence. the one she could turns to when in pain from cramps, or to get consolation for a not so good of a day
She often cried and complained to her at times about why she'd not been born a boy.

youth's mysteries bloom,
fear and courage intertwined,
womanhood's embrace.

the society

the body she wore

judgment on her waist size and thigh,.
like bartering fruits
the smaller they are,
the better they declare
reducing her worth to mere numbers, unfair.

a smaller waist, they would insist,
fits right to the box,
society's mold, they imposed on her
pressuring her to fit, unfair

if she's plump, they asked to be thin,
complexions judged by their own scale.
each moment
scrutinized, criticized,
the assessments,
she couldn't abide.

her body, entirely hers to mend,
her look, her choice,
no one should dictate how she's displayed,
her potential is a huge ocean,
not to be swayed.

-to the criticising minds

judgements she never wanted

she wasn't the timid girl you see
she has the fire inside her
as time passed by
she started to live in fear
her life had become a terror

they killed her dreams
her zill to live
made her doubt herself
if she is enough
for anything!

she screamed her dreams
begged to fly high
again and again
but instead of support and care,
only judgments filled the air.

she surrendered to their decree,
she gave in to the cruelty
a puppet to
what they wanted her to be

feeling of belonging

some said
girls are precious
they would protect her
raise her right
in every step of her life

she thought
she belongs to her parents
who nurtured her in life's embrace,
given her mere existence

now she must adapt
into another family's orbit,
because society says, that's it!
but who are they to commit?

who gets to decide?
to whom she belongs?
she's not a thing to be implied,
or to be forced upon on someone
why is her identity being questioned?

stop treating her
as a trading subject
just to prove your worth to society
she's not a puzzle piece to be thrown,
she belongs to herself alone.

she's not someone to be given away,
to please others in any way,
she knows where she'll stay,
her belonging is her own ray.

the urge of proving herself

she will always go
that extra mile
to make people happy
to bring smiles,
or prove herself of being
a great mom, sister, wife maybe

why is it that
she wants a validation!
for the things she does
but does not get the same in return

she'd give up all, without a sight,
for the ones she cares about,
living only for them,
in roles that feel just right.

in her heart, a strong desire,
for some recollection of her sacrifices
that will come in her way
for the love she gives day by day.

the little girl's cry

she stood there, numb.
not sure what just happened, not sure at all.
she didn't know what to say or do,
who to talk to,
or how to get through.
she thought she'd be safe,
around those she trusted,
but her little heart didn't understand,
the darkness lurking from behind.

people asked,
why she got quiet
what could she say?
he closed her mouth, to stop her scream,
slipped through her dress,
left her aching each moment
cruelty took over, a horrifying night.

the dress kept hidden

she loved and accepted
her body
the way it is
a thicker thigh or
higher waist size
couldn't dull her free-spirited rise.

she wore that special dress,
bought with a joyful heart,
set off with the biggest smile
colors echoed her soul's grace,
peachy pink just like her face

as she walked out,
a few voices she heard,
noticing the softness 'round her waist,
the marks of life on her thighs.
they scrutinized her chest's size,
and her bulky arms, like a man
sturdy and strong,
her open flowing hair
to them, it all felt somehow wrong.

all she wished for was simple,
that pretty dress she wanted to wear
but their words left her nothing but pain,
not be able to look at her body
not wanting it anymore
no longer she wanted to be the same.

so, she concealed that dress,
locked away a part of her true essence,
fighting to match her inner self,
with a world of false pretense.

-to those who scrutinized

flag bearer of feminism

they called her a feminist,
when she stood strong
for what she wanted,
not afraid to share her story,
of a lifelong struggle.

she had to work twice as hard,
to prove herself in this patriarchal world.
balancing family and work,
because that's what was expected, they said

her dreams were kept on hold,
so others could have a better future.
she left her home and her past,
to only meet society's demands.

whether labelled a feminist or not,

they simply aimed to tag her,

and silence her voice,

suppress her,

for merely seeking what's rightfully hers.

she's had enough,

she won't have it anymore.
putting herself first,

her needs and rights at the core.

no longer just a woman, she's a human first, and much more.

-to the girls who speaks for her rights

the trauma that took her

claiming ownership of another
through a marriage
does not mean to possessing their soul,
it's not merely the body,
it's the spirit dwelling within.

he laid hands on her,
whenever he pleased,
unmindful of her desires,
believing she was exclusively his,
solely because he was the household's man,
providing for her needs.

forcing himself upon her,
fed his weird sense of masculinity,
leaving her broken day by day,
desiring escape,
perhaps even death,
to break free from this torment.

all the dreams she once held,
of a joyous married life,
now appear as far as distant.
she sought assistance,
only to be offered advice of
compromise and adjustment.

it was society that enforced her,
being with someone
who regarded her as only a possession,
not a person.
they brainwashed her,
that this is how norms are
how things functioned within a marriage.

she accepted,
compelled herself to believe,
this was the path her life must follow.
only one day she gave up
she could face no more
she choose to end a life of suffering
and leave the pain behind forever

survivor is she?

She survived, not just death, but the torment that tore her soul apart. She lived the agony of rape, treated as a mere object for someone else's satisfaction. The physical wounds healed, but the scars on her soul remained, haunting her.

Every time she looked at herself, panic engulfed her. It all began with stalking and bullying, and she was told to ignore it, merely because she was the girl.

Started to eve teasing, it escalated to groping on public transport, yet she was still expected to ignore it.

But even her resilience couldn't deter them. They aimed to crush her body and spirit with their desires.

She made it through all of that, but deep down, did she really survive at all?

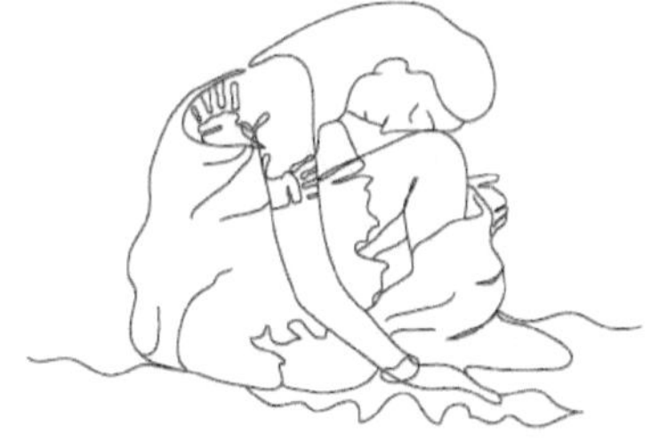

never ending march of equality

half of her life now,
she knows this fight,
it won't be done,
but she'll keep on trying, one by one.

she'll convince them all,
that equal respect, it's not denied,
for she can do
just what a man can do,
give her a chance,
she'll prove it's true.

she wants their trust,
from the people she love,
equality's not a battle to wage,
it's a necessity for this age.

no need for politics, or big debates,
the change can come
only by you people
right, in your own home.

her unforeseen endless struggle

countless years,
don't you think?
her story of hardship,
isn't finished yet,
and it won't be ending soon.

she kept on fighting,
time and again,
proving her worth,
for all that required.

be it the battlefield or
when family needed her the most,
she never failed to amaze.
and she'll keep doing just that.
until the day she lives

because she believes on
that hope of light,
she knows
she's meant for greater things.

the "self" she wanted

she has a different body
different than the usual
they put her in a box
told her how to be
or even how to feel

a man is what they wanted her to be
who can protect and provide
strong and secure,
but inside she felt different
it's the womanhood
that she craved
she longed to be her true nature

being herself as a woman felt right,
she tried, explained
how she felt
inside the wrong body,
her path was tough,
her life became a journey,
rugged and rough.

she just wanted to live
the way she is
without people disgusting upon her
without judgment, without being frowned,
was it her fault!
for speaking what her soul soared?

she knows her worth

they spoke of a tradition,
trading their son for what they want
dowry is what they call it
getting a daughter along with it
it was beyond her thought anyway
she could never accept it

she didn't agree
to what they say
she is
not an item to give or convey,
not an object, to bargain or chain,
to be treated like merchandise,
it is insane.

she will walk away
right at that moment
leave it to her
she will show you
what she can do
it's her worth
that you need to accept, you fool.

-to the so-called tradition

burned her soul

why is it that
she is forced upon
everything in life
like a puppet nothing less

if she didn't like
someone teasing her
or calling her names
she gave a tight slap
on his face
because it's what
they all deserve anyways

unaware of the consequences
she thought
she made him silent
not just her face
her soul too burnt that day
when her skin squeezed with acid drops
and people watched away

hide herself?

hide yourself,
don't reveal who you are,
or they'll judge you,
till you lose your will to live.

hide your scars and bruises,
to be a good wife,
so they can display it to the world.

keep your bra straps hidden,
or they'll call you careless.

cover your sanitary pads,
or they'll say you're shameless.

dont show too much skin,
or they'll brand you a slut.

what's wrong with you all?
isn't it enough?
she had to fight with you,
just to be born,
she has to fear you,
over and over again.

the friendship

in friendship's dance

from borrowed pens and classroom gossip,
to continuous laughter shared, falling on the floor.
irritating each other grew when boredom's near,

from dressing up each other,
to becoming lifelines, you, and me.
we've come so far,
in friendship's dance,

i wish it stays like this forever

we grew so was our friendship

the smiles and fights

i remember those innocent smiles,
and even our silly fights
it's always you and me
in my heart,
the memories, they'll never depart.

i know you are busy in life
it's difficult to reach out
sometime ego and pride
also plays its part
and friendships fall out

i dont blame the distance
neither you nor me
maybe it was the time
not right for both of us, you see

shoulder to cry on

She was always there when I needed a shoulder to lean on, whether it was over something silly or a heartbreak that weighed on me. Those weren't easy times, but when we both bitched about the same person, it felt like we were equally carrying the burden, and I felt a bit lighter.

I'm not typically one to share my feelings openly, but she's more of a talkative type.

So, it became her turn to listen, and she did just that. She listened as I poured my heart out in front of her, offering no comments or judgments, just a caring ear willing to hear my thoughts and worries.

the long talks

i called my friend one day, you see,
just to vent and feel less cranky.
but when she picked up the line,
i could tell something wasn't fine.

i asked her
what's going on in your mind,
and she started talking,
nonstop
for hours,
she talked stories,

in detail, so vast,
from her work colleague
to clothes that won't fit,
she went on so fast.

i hung up,
feeling a bit surprised,
i'd called to unload,
and realized.
instead, her stories took over,
but i guess
that's what friends are for.

she knew

when i told her
about this boy i'd found,
she already knew,
she was always around.
my blushing cheeks and my phone's ring,
told her everything,
every little thing.

she waited for
the time that's right,
to say she's happy,
with heart so light.
she wasn't ready to speak her part,
but she knew he'd captured my heart.

She watched my life,
not to intrude or chide,
Just to make sure,
I didn't slide, into love's depths, foolishly,
She cared, you see, about me.

the friendship's test

she'd take me places
i didn't like,
even though i'd rather
stay out of sight.
but thanks to her, i'd see the sun's glow,
each morning,
waiting for class to go.

she was a lazy ass
trust me it's true,
making me wait for hours
in the heating sun
maybe she was testing
our friendship's bounds

looking back
it's clear as water
she just wanted to check on me
to see if i remain firm,
lady, you wait
now it's your turn

-to that friend

precious memories

the love we once knew,
was meant
to always stay true.
but time has made us drift,
in life's intricate,
evolving script.

feelings linger, no doubt,
life's busyness
made us apart.
priorities shifted,
roles changed,
hope our friendship will stay
unaltered, unchanged.

from living nearby, close as,
to creating tales of children we'd win.
in these memories, forever we'll confide,
cherishing moments, hearts open wide.

the moments we have spent
from planning to buy
house near to each other
so will never have to separate, ever!!

to making up stories
on how our children will look like
a true friendship is defined
not on the days to count
rather on the moments we shared

moments of laughter

it's such a release,
to tease,
saying silly things,
and making up
weird stories

our entertainment,
indeed,
a nightly need,
giggles and grins spread wide,
as we share memories we recite.

gossip about people we dislike,
brings laughter,
what a hike!
in this fun banters we find,
moments of joy, i tell you
one of a kind.

always there

he was always around,
when i needed to
let off some steam, i found.
though we didn't talk much,
months could pass,
but his care was such.

when i called him,
he would always hear,
to hear about life,
and make my worries disappear.
long talks filled with
laughter and fun banter,
in those moments, i felt him near.

even if i said life was tough,
that things were
rough and feeling gruff,
he'd chuckle,
trying to make things light,
but deep inside, i knew he cared, alright.

lost connections: threads of time

In the tale of "what if", there's a missing thread—a phone call we never shared, and a web of misunderstanding that destroyed our connection. If I could rewind the time, I wish for a clearer mind and a heart more mature to mend the fences, to take back the sharp words we said to each other.

Time, relentless and unforgiving, has sculpted us in its own way. Life's trials and turbulences have forged us into who we are today. Maybe I have changed throughout the course of time because of some situations, and so have you. And i have accepted the fact that even though we talk or dont it's not going to end. I hope it does not.

The respect I have for the moments spend will always stay and will try to always be there for you no matter what. It might take some time to narrow the gap between us.

But to cherish your happy moments with you. To hype you in your high and support you on your lows, will always be there!

What else friends are for right!

-to the lost friendship

the love

newness of youth

they said she's grown, no more a child,
inside, she felt the change, a bit wild.

adapting, questioning, her feelings,
her body transformed, a new look compiled.

the gazes, she noticed,
emotions surged, like waves, roared.

discovering herself, each passing day
boys' stares, something new, she observed.

fluttering butterflies

a friend's gentle voice,
a secret did she say,
of butterflies and love in a mystic way.
in her thoughts, wings of hope flew,
longing for love,
in a waiting que.

the love's sweet song,
she is yet to hear,
in her mind, the music was crystal clear.
her heart, like a bird, took flight,
in the hope of love's pure, radiant light.

the feeling above all

lost in her book, little she knew
life surprised her in a way
she met someone, that day
eyes locked,
and her heart skipped a bit.
it's you,
about to entangle her life with

unaware feelings began to stir,
when eyes met
a hint of something, so true.
a moment where her heart spoke to her

a path untraveled,
she'll soon embark
all that her heart say,
this next step ahead
its love
that people say..

love came knocking

from glancing looks
to staring your photo
for hours
pondering what life would become
crafting a love poem

waiting for your message
to talking for hours
knitting dreams together
love was all around the air

hand-holding to endless chats,
to siting, talking, and laughing
hours flew by
from the foods we liked
to buying a house together
the future seemed
sheer clear

the feeling of belonging
was all we wanted
ready to face the world,
the love we claimed.
hearts entangled, an unbreakable fetter,
in love's embrace, we would face any weather.

symphony of love

no melodies of a violin in the air,
no love songs,
no cupid's arrow,
it all seems like a scene from a movie, you see,
but when love happens,
that's when it all feels free.

only then do you truly understand,
that something beautiful has taken over your life
in your life,
it weaves its tender art,
and fills your world with warmth from the heart.

in the moments shared,
in each sweet embrace,
love paints a picture, a smile on your face,
with every glance, a new chapter turns,
in the story of love,
where hearts and dreams encounters.

-to love

invisible threads of love

talking for hours,
eagerly waiting for each other's message
never wanting to say goodbye.
has its own charm in time,

They both stalked each other's profiles, being the first to like pictures and send birthday wishes. Waiting at the bus stop just to share a five-minute walk. Telling little lies to friends to hang out together and picking each other's favorite dishes at restaurants, whenever they went out to eat.

all of it adds up to the blush on her cheeks every time she sees him.

these moments hold a special connection, filling their hearts with a warm feeling that words can't express.

lost in silence

the silence is what bothered
she asked for reasoning
again and again
and you only ignored

the silence filled up
with distance and fights,
and turned into
heartbreak one night

it was never about
the disagreements
it was your attitude,
always wanting an
escape from the problems

the pause

it wasn't news to her though,
she knew,
you were slipping away,
falling out of love
leaving her behind, all alone,

"moving on" to a life that's new,
breaking her, piece by piece,
letting her mourn and weep
left her hanging,
asking for help, seeking escape

had it been the opposite
she would never
leave you
she knows the love
in her heart
moments she cherished
she holds so close
it wasn't just a casual fling,
she fell for you,
for her,
love is a real thing.

the night

holding her close
you whispered in her year
it's you and me
nothing else i crave, my dear

"if i could stop the moment
i would hold it right here"
the smell of her body
that you could smell so clear

the honey wrapped words
you told her that day
she believed it all
it was nothing but
all a lie,
when it was revealed to her
she could do nothing but cry

crying, sobbing, mourning
for nights on the same bed
scrolling through your messages
that you had left on seen,

holding her pillow tight
the sheets were half wet
her tears could not stop
she could not breathe.

the night became darker
embracing the emptiness
inside her,
she held close, all the things you left
she clung to her phone,
wishing you would be with her

the flashbacks

Why is it that in between everyday things. Just passing by a normal day. Living my life, and there comes a moment when i realize taking that spoon to my mouth or walking down the stairs or waiting for my bus ,is that you are gone from my life, long gone.

That moment just transports me back to years, leaves me thinking about you. Wishing for the time to go back and let me rewrite the story.

It was you who i wanted, yes you. But i was just a nameless "someone" for you, that's all. What shattered me was not because you walked away, choose to have things in a simpler way, not to fight for love, not to fight for me. it's the mere fact that, two people who promised to spend the rest of the time of their life with each other. have just become some flashbacks in time that comes and goes but leaves me heartbroken every time.

it was all she wanted

she wanted
a passionate lover
or even a
die-hard romantic
just like in the movies

she would plan
for the surprise
or even let you
take over her body at night

she would blush
listening to your voice
or reading your text
she would not say it often
but she cares

everything was a lulu buy
until she knew
it was her respect
getting torn
she was giving
too much of herself
and not expecting the same in return

love is like a dream
she wants to dive right in
but respect is
what she deserves
in every instant of her existence

believing she could fix this time

She thought she could fix it this time, just like every other time when you messed up. All she ever did was try to mend things, even though she knew a part of her was slowly slipping away in the process. She wasn't quite ready to give up on you yet.

She held onto hope like a lifeline in turbulent seas, believing in the possibility of change. But deep inside, she felt her heart growing thinner. Still, for the sake of love, she clung to that flicker of hope.

warmth of hope
in a fading heart's wish,
love's fragility.

-to the fragile love

a half-written poem

she felt a change deep inside
all for the sake of love,
when her heart wanted cozy nights,
you sought parties and city lights.
she craved conversations, rich and deep,
about art, and poems,
and secrets to keep,
she wanted you, but you never care.

she'd eat your choice,
though it made her sick,
just to watch you,
with a childlike flair

all she wanted was
to hold your hand in front of the world
to declare her love for you
to show you off to the universe

it was difficult for you to see
appreciate her beauty
in her simplicity

her love
will now forever stay in her poem
never to come out for anyone
ever again

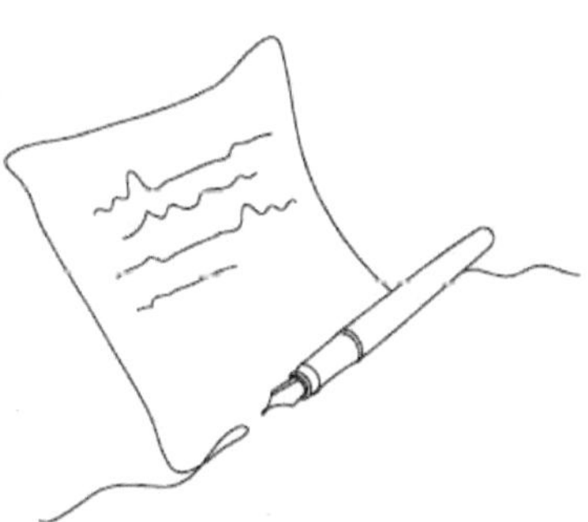

her love language

In the quiet of the evening, you turned to me with a question, "How can you love me so much?" Your eyes searched for answers in the depths of my soul.

I replied with a gentle smile, "It's because I stumbled upon you when I wasn't even searching for someone. Love didn't strike me like just like that; instead, it grew steadily over the years. It's no longer just you and me; it's 'us' now. A beautiful fusion of two souls, entwined by shared experiences and emotions."

'Us' having the beautiful, shared moments, sipping tea together, feelings we've told to each other that have not shared with anyone else, and that one love song that resonated with both of us instantly, those moments siting silently yet knowing exactly what both of us are thinking.

The thousands poems i written for you just to see you listen to those and smile, the tea you made for me the first time,

the laugh you have for my child like happiness around deserts, and your warm hug when i feel like giving up It's all of this.

So how could I not love all these and how could i not love you?"

the longing

she's trying to let go,
missing the love she once knew.

a love gone wrong,
cut her deep,
left her hurt,
unable to sleep.
it sliced her soul, made her cry,
left her alone, wondering why.

still, she longs for what's lost,
a love that came at a heavy cost.

her gut aches
when she hears your name,
in an empty room,
she hides her pain.

she cries for hours until feeling numb,
longing for the love that's long gone.

the feeling in her poem remains the same,
a love lost, a lingering flame.

the baggage of sorrow

the baggage of sorrow
she carries along with her
it's just too heavy to let go now

feeling tired of hearing voices
to be strong
dragging the baggage on her way
she still smiles and shows
she is okay!!

she is getting torn
day by day,
the shadow of darkness
taking her away...

"depression's just a phase,"
they said,
yet it still continues, unchanged,
why does it stay,
so deep, so wide,

leaving her trapped
unable to hide,
in a troubled mind, a beautiful heart is confined?
leaving her body
was only option she had
to end the suffering
the aching heart,
no one looked deep in her eyes.
ever to understand,
it was just too much for her
her silent cries
cry for help
went unnoticed to everyone.

life's circle

You didn't care when I asked for changes or tried to make things better for us. I believed in you and us, even when things were tough. I just want to understand why it seems so easy for you to move on. Was everything we had a lie? It's hard to believe.

But the person I see now makes me sad, not for you but for the person you used to be,

for losing the one who never gave up on you, no matter how many times you hurt me.

Now, I blame myself for letting you hurt my feelings like this. What kind of person are you? Is it so simple for you to move on without thinking about the person who was there for you?

I hope things turn out differently for you, but if karma catches up with you someday, maybe it's what you deserve.

the demons she fought

the demons
she fought inside her
was ready to take her over,
the evil laugh
she could hear.

they said
give up my darling
you fight is over,
closed the doors behind
screams harder and harder.

it's not just her body
het soul is what they wanted,
the vulnerability of her heart
is what they seek.

choking in her own breath
she kept asking for help,
but there was no one there
only the void he left.

moment of truth

she saw it clear as day,
when she begged for love
from those who never understood
her hearts way,
those who never cared to stay,
as she wandered, come what may.

she has given it all
every single time,
just to be put in to
this paradigm,
she's asking for what she's due,
all the love, pure and true.

trust, faith, the care that she showered
yet it's her heart you broke,
did you think you're to be forgiven?
to treat her heart with such neglect,
you will face the consequences
you are not to be escaped.

life is a circle, you know
it comes full round
you reap what in life's field is found,

she got the hint of reality
of the difference between
love and need
or is it just convenience you seek!

the moment of truth
went right through her,
cut through like a sword
when her dreams shattered
revealed the side of a monster.

done with you

she no longer
yearns for you
wants you or crave you
desire you,
you're no longer a part of her life's view,
she's done with your games,
that much is true.

the dumps of
sorrows
you left for her
the scars you
scratched again and again
just to make her feel that pain

the words you uttered
so bluntly, it meant nothing to you
in the end,
it was all a lie for you
she was just a body

with flesh and bone
for that matter !!
it was all a facade for you
i am sure.

you dug a hole
in her soul,
deep within
only and only
insecurities brawl.

the melancholy love

love hurts
it breaks, burns, and shatters you
it's not for those hearts are weak
the war it brings with,
you will see
is never easy to fight

it does takes you to heaven
to show you the beautiful side
through moments tough,
it seeks to know,
if you're deserving,
if your love can grow.

love will test you
on the moments
it wants you to prove
you are worthy of the divine feeling
through ups and downs,
we come to know,
love's sweet melancholy
helps us grow.

so, in love's bittersweet movie scenes,
we find where we truly belong.
in its sadness, we discover grace,
love's melancholy, in our hearts,
finds its place.

story of the night

Opening her diary that day, a whirlwind of thoughts swirled in her mind, begging to be unleashed onto paper. Retrieving an old diary from the depths of her drawer, concealed beneath a pile of work papers, she took a deep breath. The box of emotions, hidden away for so long, was now ready to be opened.

As she started writing, the night stilled, as if holding its breath to witness and live each moment with her. Her heart's longing to converse with her old friend, "the diary," had finally been granted.

Together, they delved into the depths of her unspoken words, unveiling the fragments of her soul that had remained concealed from the world. Returning to the same old house, filled with the remnants of a love that had long faded, was painful for her. Today, she was determined to release it all, to share with someone who would simply listen and understand the pain she was going through.

With each emotion she poured onto the pages, she felt a sense of liberation, as if soaring through the sky like a bird set free. As she revisited her written tale, she realized it was time to conclude the old chapter and embark on a new story.

the night waited patiently,
eager to hear her tale unfold,
in the sacred pages of her diary.

the life

life unfolded

life unfurled
infront of her
choosing herself or love?
she must decide for her,
she had to pick this time around
to safeguard her inner voice,
above all
her innocence heart's essence

life offered her a new start
to live life in her own part,
this time
not to bid love adieu
but to love herself first.

her heart spoke to her

she wished he'd stay with her,
fight for the love they shared.
but it seemed too simple, you see,
maybe his love wasn't as pure as it should be.

who could walk away like this
it broke her into million pieces
this time her heart cried out,
"step back, don't linger in self-doubt.

it's not you, my dear,
it's him who leaves,
love remains within you,
in your heart it begins.
people leave, but love will always stay
just the person departing,
don't lose your way."

-to the one who got hurt

the hustle bustle

she struggled
for the little things
to calm her
chaotic mind.
leaving things behind,
wasn't easy for her
neither to accept things
the way they are.

every time
her eyes would water,
she would promise herself
to hustle harder

she found peace
in the hustle bustle of life,
it only made her
forget her pain
make her feel alive.

the little moments

the times
she spent
with the little dog on the street
or chatting with a stranger she'd meet
brewing her own cup of tea,
reviving old hobbies, happy and free.

long talks with a close friend,
walks by the sea
without any fear,
feeling the calmness
the peace she sought had reappeared.

life's surprises,
so subtly designed,
in these little moments,
realizing here's more to unwind,
a brighter future is what
she's inclined.

overthinker to optimistic

She struggled, an overthinker, always picturing the worst. Anxiety made her fret over imagined problems, even small ones.

Innocence was her gift, a childlike heart. Today, she hums a peace tune, ready for life's challenges. She treasures these moments, embracing life's ups and downs.

Panic still stirs within, but she hides it well. She's learned to handle conflicts, smiling through it all. She's optimistic, guarding her life's story from others now.

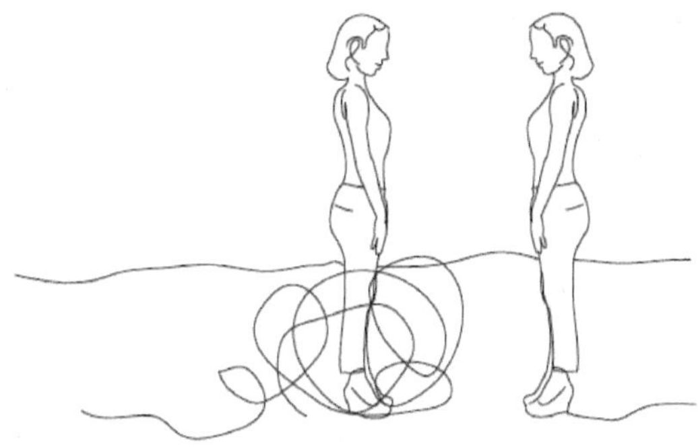

opening a blank canvas

in the depths of her sorrow,
through heartbreak's pain,
her colors had died.
a blank canvas,
not easily could she find,
she struggled through, her strength unchained.

a tunnel dark,
a hellish hole,
but she fought through,
with heart and soul.
emerging into the light so bright,
her canvas filled with colors,
she found herself smiling again
she found the light inside.

opening a new chapter,
her spirit revoked,
with a heart so kind.
in life's canvas,
her story moved,
with each brushstroke,
you witness her,
painting the portrait of her soul,
through her, a divine glow unfurls.

innocence of emotions

emotions, they dance, so free, you see?
not caring of what should be,
they arrive, then depart,
like a fleeting dream,
in joy or sorrow
they're not what they seem.

happy or sad,
beyond tears and laughter,
to make you human, they claim,
emotions, is the heart's language,
its unique name.

the feelings you sense,
a heart's sweet view,
guiding you through life's rollercoaster,
the journey it crafts,
just for you.

mending herself

she wove herself into different shades,
with each passerby,
adapting like a chameleon
but now, she yearns for her true hue,
to recapture the essence of what she once knew.

time to time, she adjusted her core,
moulding herself,
always wanting to give more,
but now she regrets those shifts and turns,
wishing for her old self,
the one that burns.

the old her, so innocent and free,
before life's complexity came to be,
she longs for the days of unbroken dreams,
to mend herself back, to sew life's seams.

in the tapestry of time,
reweave the fabric of her heart, now widespread,
yearning for the past's blissful, gentle scent,
mending herself to be whole,
to feel truly content.

echoes of piece

The soft morning light shines through the curtains and gently wakes her up. She wishes to wake up to a world filled with the things she loves the most. She dreams of a special place where her dreams come true in bright and beautiful ways, and where she always has a happy smile on her face.

In this dream world, she keeps her heart safe, so no one can hurt it. It's like a cozy hideaway where she feels peaceful. She sits by an open window, listening to the soothing sound of raindrops, which makes her feel calm. She holds a book in one hand and a hot cup of coffee in the other, enjoying the smell of the coffee.

Here, in this timeless dreamland, the music she loves never gets old, and it always makes her feel good. She has said goodbye to people who didn't appreciate her and who made her sad. Now, she's true to herself and shines like a star. In her dreams, she gets everything she wants, keeps her smile, and loves herself deeply.

One day she wishes this dream of her come true!!

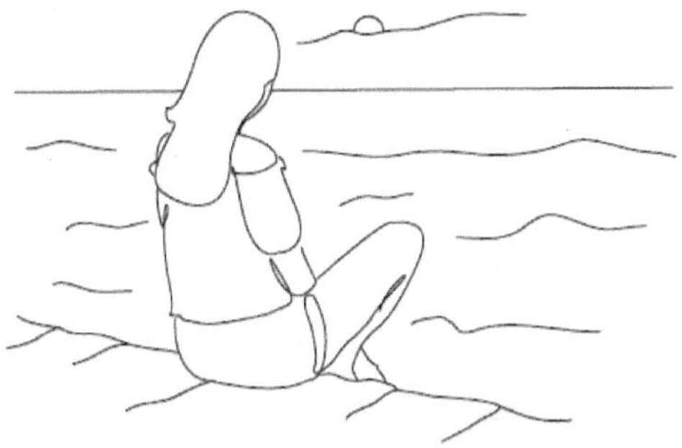

shredding into a new her

her heart felt trapped,
a hell hole
a pit of her own past
a place unknown
the key to unlock it, long gone,

through the marsh of sorrow and sadness
dragging herself out
she told herself, “i shall live,
the finest years,
no need for any magical affair.
i’m ready to confront each trial,

work on dreams i once set aside,
never giving up again, i’ll seize the day,
it’s time to rise, shine bright,
and make my way.
i’ll leave a mark in every heart,
whatever come may.

forgotten pieces of life

She forgot who she was, trying to be what someone else wanted. She didn't realize what she was missing until she finally stepped out of her self-imposed walls. It felt like entering a whole new world, and though she was afraid at first, she understood that this was her reality now.

she knew she had to gather herself
to face it,
to fight it
to live it this time
only for herself

forgiving self in love's torment

love has not been kind to her
she went through the torment
just to feel the love again
it left a scar in her heart
wrenched her soul's terrain,
she ended up with
the self-blame game.

deep within the sorrow's pit
she found a ray of hope
a new found grace
to forgive herself
to mend her spirit
to rekindle her life.

the scars remain
she wore them with grace,
to a testament of
love's unkind phase.

in love's torment
healing love's wounds
forgiving herself
the spirit reborn,
it's not love anymore
that the heart wants.

setting her spirit free

she wanted to be free at last,
no more pain,
to feel joy and peace in her soul again.
after all the fights
life's cruel sting,
she longed for life's embrace
she wished a new beginning.

even with a heart that fell part half,
she'd start anew,
healing her wounded soul.
now, she's complete,
with self-love's sweet touch,
her spirit soars high in a happy place.

in the mirror,
she sees a warrior in herself,
setting her spirit free
manifesting better days.

-to her, who wants to fly high

heart's boundaries defined

In the tale of her life, she once hung to threads of vulnerability, allowing others to encroach upon her self-respect. But time has unveiled a transformation. Walls no longer guard her, yet boundaries stand tall, a testament to her newfound strength.

She respects those around her, yet she has learned to honour herself above all. Love remains in her heart, though it resides in a chamber protected by the lessons of the past.

The fairy tales of yesteryears have faded. She now scripts her own narrative, living life on her own terms. Those who failed to acknowledge her feelings have faded into the background, their absence is now insignificant.

As the burdens lifted, a subtle light glows within her, casting a warm glow on the path she now confidently walks.

in life's tapestry,
boundaries guard newfound strength,
a self-love revealed.

in pursuit of self

love, with its quirky sense of humour,
she grasped it a tad too late, the rumour.
she should've loved herself first,
but in the name of love,
she was forced,
into a messy situation,
she couldn't reverse.

life turned into an unknown land,
leaving people behind,
she chose herself.
she went down a path alone,
knowing it might be a lonely,
she just wasn't ready for another fight,
so she decided
to hold her feelings tight.

it seemed easy
to hide them now,
to keep her moments to herself.
the emotions she once held close,
now reside in a locked heart's shadow.
she's chosen
not to let them free,
they'll stay hidden for eternity.

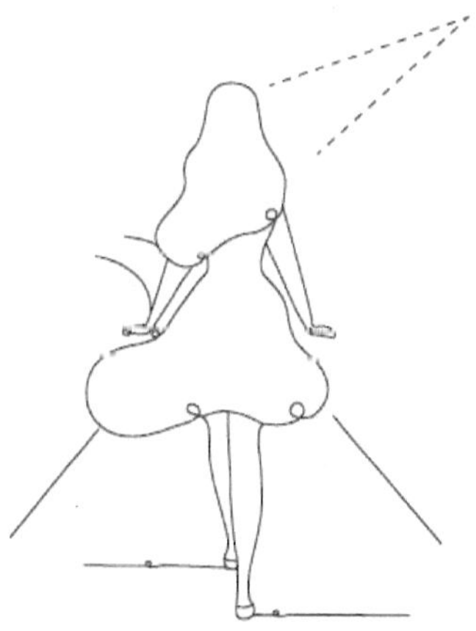

writing her destiny

She's on a path to find herself, searching for answers. She's given a lot, but sometimes, she didn't get much in return. As she explores her feelings, she finds an emptiness from people who've come and gone.

She's strong, and her emotions are vivid and intense. It's either all or nothing for her.

But now, she realizes she's not here to be controlled by others. She's determined to make her mark in the world.

heart talk

heart to heart

Family

I think family is the one thing that you cannot change in life. It is is who you are born with, your blood relation, and sometimes at the end of the road you will find only them standing by you no matter who else is there. People come and go you see, but family will stay always.

When you are born into a family from shaping your thought process to imparting values on you, the kind of person you become in the future depends on the family members you have around. Depending on the kind of things you listen to while growing up, consciously or unconsciously it makes a big impact on the person you are becoming in the process.

We say whatever you teach a child stays with them for the rest of their life. And maybe that's why our parents are so protective of us about what kind of influence they want on us while growing up. Every parent dreams of giving a life to their children that they never had or even giving the best that they can at the moment.

All parents have seen their fair share of struggle while trying to make a living for them and trying to give the best possible thing to their children. Working hard every day not for them, but for the child to have an easy life. That's the kind of love our parents have for us, doing everything for us silently in their own way and making sure to never make us feel we are missing something in life.

To the father who silently handles all the finances, saving each penny and thinking a thousand times before spending on himself, only to give his children a good education. Calculates a thousand permutations before taking any crucial decision as he knows the whole family is dependent on him, sacrificing things that he might want but instead buying them for their children.

He shows off his child's success in front of people, yet won't overhype them to keep them grounded.

I know they lack a little when it comes to showing their love and care.

But I know that they care, they care a lot. They care enough to wait for you till you come home, they care enough to check on you if you have reached safely, if you are travelling. They care enough to ask you if you need anything even when you are embarrassed to ask. I say thank you and I love you to all those fathers.

To the mom who crushed her bone literally to bring her child into this world. Starting from smiling at your silly tantrums to teaching lessons about life. Making sure you don't fall sick to taking care of you and sitting by you all night. Not thinking about what food she wants to eat, to making your favourite food to eat when you come back home. Packing stuff when you are travelling and calling a thousand times to stop overthinking and imagining the worst that could happen. From helping you study to have tears in her eyes at each successful step of in your life. From teaching you the right and wrong path in life to standing up for you when you are in trouble. She has grown up with you too.

We say the bond between a child and a mother is above all, above anything in this world. This is so true. Over the course of time, we all realize it, we realize her in our life, but yet never express it, and even if we do, it will never be enough.

To all those moms who made their children their life,

I say I love you to all those mothers.

You know, It's only when you start living your life independently, specially without your parents, then you realize the value of those life lessons that your parents taught you, you realize how important those little moments that you had spent with them, and the kind of person you have become to live a life of your own and everything you have now along with it, which was possible only and only because of your parents.

PS: will always be grateful to God for being born with an amazing parents

heart to heart

Friends

Do you remember the first friend you made in your life? That feeling must be so precious right!

And do you remember that friend who spent hours with you talking, laughing, or even crying with you. Do you have that friend still with you, do you still talk and laugh at each other's silly habits, like the way you talk or the way you eat or the way you get angry on little things, or the way you hit each other just for fun.

If Yes! Then let me tell you you are very lucky to have that person in your life. If you have them by your side to pick up the phone call at 3 am at night and ramble about your midnight thoughts and the laugh at each other's problems. Then you have someone you should not let go off ever!!

I think friend is someone who sometimes acts like your mother when they are too much protective about you, can act like a father and come to save you when you are in trouble, can act like a sibling to fight with you on silly things, and act like a lover to love you to any extent in their one way. But the thing is they are always there, they are there to listen to your complaints, to console you, to hug you, to hold you close, even to shout at you sometimes if they find you loosing yourself along the way.

They are there to celebrate your small achievements as if it's their own, to cry with you when you are going through something. They are there to laugh with you and make you smile when you dont even want to talk. We say half of your problems in life are solved if you have someone to talk your heart out with and to let go of the burden, and that's when you need a friend you know!

I know we all get busy in our lives, and priorities changed, being in that rat race sometimes makes us forget the relationship we have around, and sometimes we lose them along the way. But the bond is never lost, the moments are not gone. Cherish the little moments you have spent with each other every now and then. You never know when is the next time you are going to see them.

Friendship is kind of a unique relationship i feel, it does not just come and go like that. When it comes into your life it brings all the laughter, smiles, fun, silliness and when it leaves it takes with a part of you along with it. Break ups in a friendship is much more hurting than losing a lover

It's just you miss someone who was supposed to be there with you, and you do want to be there with each other, but a wall comes in between called ego. I understand that is because sometimes we expect too much because we love too much.

But keep that aside for now, call that friend, ask them how they are doing, ask them if they are ok, until the point they are ready to open their heart out to you again. Don't let the beautiful moments wash away just like that, hold on to them and bring them back, they are your own.

All of us should have that friend or be that friend to someone in our life who never lets go of you no matter what. If you have that friend already thank them for being there with you all this time.

heart to heart

Love

Oh you sweet love,

In your magical world of love where the emotions run deep, and heart starts beating faster than ever for that person. It's sweet, beautiful, and so full of excitement. Those butterflies in the stomach, the excitement, those stolen eye contacts, those moments of relief after seeing someone. All of it feels like being in the garden of heaven. To be in love is that feeling when you are falling free from high above the sky. Your body gently floating in the air, weightless and carefree.

These moments cannot be translated to words I know. You take people to heaven without wings, you show them the world filled with rainbows and butterflies with holding hand of their lover and spending an eternity in the blink of an eye. And in those moments that person falls for your sneaky little tricks.

You are kind of are like a drug you know, once someone falls in love, they just can't enough of you, isn't that right!

Love comes with its own sweet travellers of confusion,

uncertainty, and guilt, but they are there just to add a twist to your story, love has its unique way of making up your story worth watching, and breaking it up when it feels you have not lived up to it.

But, my love, there's a shadow that sometimes hides beneath your radiant facade. Why do you often keep the pain and heartbreak hidden behind the scenes? It's as if you reveal only one side of the coin, and I wonder why.

You have taken me on quite a journey i can say, I wouldn't trade a single second of our journey. I wonder if that's what was in store for me, or you just thought of testing my kindness and thought of teaching me a lesson. When i was searching for love all around, begging for it even after all the drama. All i had to do is look inside!

It was all inside me all along!

My dearest love, you are a paradox—a blend of joy and pain, of laughter and tears. And while you may challenge me at times, I am grateful for the profound depth you've added to my life.

The twists and turns you throw my way, has definitely been my path corrector in life. Shaping me to be the person i am today, let me give you some credit, actually no, a lot of credit, for teaching me not to give that precious love to someone who just puts up a face and nothing less in the name of love. To protect the love in my heart not to get washed away by the pretentious people around me.

You are the canvas upon which my heart paints its most vivid colors when i think my life is colorless, the unwavering presence that brings warmth to my soul when i start giving up on life for that matter, you are the anchor that steadies me in turbulent waters when i start to loose myself sometime, and for that, I am eternally thankful.

PS: *Thank you for making me realize the meaning of love by showing me what love is not exactly, and igniting that sweet fire of self-love in me.*

heart to heart

Note to self

Hey you listen up,

Hope you are continuing to be awesome as you are. Or at least trying to be a better person every day. thank you for keeping the promise and not giving up when situations were difficult.

I know, i know you must be questioning your choices in things and in people when you are left alone and did not get what you deserve in return, but trust me the people who left, never had the intention to stay by you, and the people who stood by are there for a reason.

Stop tormenting yourself for finding out reasons and thinking any less of you, i understand your kind heart always puts you in a dilemma when it comes to letting go of people, your mind becomes chaotic finding out reasons for everything. People might say you are sensitive towards your feelings, don't listen to them, i know it takes a lot to have an attitude of working on things and not giving up in a world full of move on and let go. Because it takes a lot of courage to stay and fight the situation and it's very easy to just give up and run away.

Don't listen to those cowards who make you feel bad about having a softer side of you, but dont give away everything of you to those people, they will never respect it, they never had. I know, i know it's been tough, and i am so proud of you for keeping the true self in you alive even after everything.

I know you might be wondering whether it was worth letting pain shatter you and giving all your love without expecting anything in return. Let me tell you those moments have made you the person you have become. You have become a stronger version of yourself. Isn't that right? I know you are tired of dealing with it all alone, but listen up, get up, dress up and be the confident woman you are. You are gorgeous inside and out. Don't let people say otherwise to you. Just make sure you live a little and enjoy the happy moments.

I hope you remember the promises we have made. It's okay sometimes to not know how to do things, take your time and figure it out for yourself. Yes, the world is crazy, and it's difficult to keep sane but you have to, trust me you are going to go places and shine bright on the eyes of those people who didn't see the light inside of you.

I am looking forward meeting you after a few years, I know you must have grown so much by then, we will rewrite this letter together then and will look back and feel proud of ourselves.

Till then surprise me with what more you have in store, believe in that superpower that is protecting you, guiding you throughout, and explore your potential, I know you are made for greater things.

PS: You are a better person than you were tomorrow, so good job to you!

About the Poet

Anindita Rath is a dynamic professional who seamlessly balances her IT career at a multinational corporation with her passion for writing. She thrives on crafting compelling narratives and sharing unique perspectives. Open to collaboration and driven by curiosity, she welcomes growth from both her personal and life experiences, making her a multifaceted individual who cherishes storytelling and approaches life as an exciting journey of discovery. You can connect with her on Instagram with the handle @scrambled.writer and explore more of her literary creations at scrambledwriter.com.

The poems symbolize life's journey—a passage through love, pain, healing, and self-discovery, embracing the different shades of life. I hope you've felt this journey through my words in these poems.

www.inkfeathers.com

We love creating beautiful books for you!

Come be a part of our ever-growing community of authors. Grow, write, and publish with us!

Scan here to explore books, authors and more

Connect with us on socials. We'd love to hear from you!

    Inkfeathers Publishing

www.ingramcontent.com/pod-product-compliance
Lightning Source LLC
LaVergne TN
LVHW041101150826
845673LV00007B/1873

* 9 7 8 8 1 1 9 4 8 3 2 8 0 *